The Christmas Miracle in *Kolendy*

HELEN GWOZDZ MILLER

WESTBOW
PRESS®
A DIVISION OF THOMAS NELSON
& ZONDERVAN

WestBow Press books may be ordered through booksellers or by contacting:

WestBow Press
A Division of Thomas Nelson & Zondervan
1663 Liberty Drive
Bloomington, IN 47403
www.westbowpress.com
1 (866) 928-1240

ISBN: 978-1-5127-7664-5 (sc)
ISBN: 978-1-5127-7663-8 (e)

Library of Congress Control Number: 2017902575

Print information available on the last page.

WestBow Press rev. date: 2/27/2017

For my husband, Frederick H. Miller,
for my children and their spouses,
and especially, for my grandchildren.

And for the members of the
Polish American Citizens Club
Whitehouse Station, New Jersey.

And for the parishioners of
Parish Community of Our Lady of Lourdes
Whitehouse Station, New Jersey.

And for the parishioners of
St. John Paul II Parish
Adams, Massachusetts.

Polish *Kolendy*

Christmas symbolizes our hope for peace and our wish to praise the birth of Christ, the prince of peace. It seems that at no other time of the year are Christian nations around the world inspired to sing with such genuine warmth and cheerfulness as at Christmas.

Through song, we express our belief in the brotherhood of man and attempt to make the world a better place to live in—a place radiating with joy and good fellowship. The Christmas we know today could not exist without the joyousness and inspiring harmonies of the carols, which serve to link us with the faith and tradition that reaches back to antiquity.

Polish Christmas carols, *kolendy*, are the musical expressions of profound religious convictions. They are not only prayers in content but also stories depicting that wondrous miracle of the nativity. Whenever the Polish family and friends gather together to enjoy the festive dinner, the *wigilia*, or *wilia*, and break the thin wafer, or *opłatek*, as an expression of brotherhood and friendliness, a captivating spirit of joy animates the members as they raise their voices in praise of the Christ child and blend them for entertainment as well. The Polish carol melodies are often based on Polish dances and songs of the peasants and of the gentry. And so, the lilting strains of the *polonaise* or the spirited measures of the *mazur* and *mazurka* lend a particular Polish and folk character to the simple, sometimes crude, but always appealing words of Polish carols. Favorite themes of the carols are the divinity and humility of our savior.

The cherished custom of singing *kolendy* reasserts itself year after year, and today it flourishes as brightly and joyously as ever, especially since we gather together to reaffirm our link to the past and understand the importance of this tradition. We perhaps are not as well versed in the language of our forefathers and may be somewhat distant from the melodic strains they offered. However, the simple act of remembering and gathering today is in itself so important. If it were not for these profound expressions that symbolize our hopes for peace and brotherhood, would reforms so important to the oppressed of Eastern Europe be a reality? Had it not been for continuing with these expressions, would this progress be made? It is important to remember the role that the Polish people have played in this progress and especially important that we understand and continue with these inspiring traditions.

- Sources unknown
(Written in 1989, based on web search sources at that time)

Acknowledgments

The greatest thanks go to my spouse, Frederick, and to our children, whose support was constant in the year 1989, when this nativity play was written. And in 2016, a thanks goes to them and to our children's spouses, for their support when I was inspired to publish it.

Thanks also go to my Christian teachers throughout my formal schooling and lifetime, and especially to the Felician Sisters, the Sisters of St. Joseph of Springfield, many diocesan priests, Jesuit priests and Benedictine priests. Learning from them has nurtured my deep Christian faith.

Special thanks go to Nadia and Bill Miller for their advice on the images selected for the book and cover. Also, a special thanks goes to Fred Miller II for his advice on the "Music Scores" chapter and to Ed Jankiewicz, who recommended Jenny Ketrow as music scores editor. Great job, Jenny! Also, thanks to Daniel Necas and Kris Kiesling at the Immigration History Research Center Archives, University of Minnesota, for their assistance in obtaining permissions for ten songs in the "Music Scores" chapter. And thanks to John Bernard Freund, CM; Tomasz Zielinski; and Fr. Rafal Kopystynski, CM, of the Eastern Province USA Vincentians, for their assistance in obtaining permissions for three songs in the "Music Scores" chapter.

Finally, thanks are extended to the many publishing experts at Westbow Press, especially to Gemma Ramos, Christopher Wolford, Chris Varquez and Rita Moore, who guided this work through the publishing process, and to Alex Stine and Larry Dale in the Editorial department, and to Bob DeGroff and staff in Publishing Services.

Preface

In the mid-1950s, in Adams, Massachusetts, for perhaps three consecutive years, the parish of St. Stanislaus Kostka, which is now part of the parish of St. John Paul II, staged productions of *jasełka(s)* or nativity plays. These were impressive, big-stage productions, and took much talent and parish-wide effort! Actors were young and old, and the productions were memorable! They made a huge impression on me, and it is in this spirit that the much smaller *jasełka*, nativity play, of this book, is offered.

Helen Gwozdz Miller
Clinton Township New Jersey
August 12, 2016

Contents

Introduction
1

Frontispiece: The "Featured" *Kolendy*
3

Nativity Play: The Christmas Miracle in *Kolendy*
7

Lyrics and Actions
23

Music Scores
33

Introduction

This is a nativity play, written in English, with *Kolendy*/hymns sung in Polish. *Kolendy* are Polish Christmas carols; see the front matter of this book for a description of Polish *Kolendy*.

Basically a tabloid is created, with actors/carolers still and statuesque, except when they are singing or acting. In the words of the two interpreters, it highlights the deep meaning and significance of the Polish *Kolendy*/hymns. It was written in 1989 and first produced on December 14, 1989. It was inspired by the Polish American Citizens Club of Whitehouse Station New Jersey, whose membership was interested in singing the *Kolendy* of its founders. Most of the members did not know Polish but remembered the melodies and struggled with the lyrics. Lyrics were syllabicated and were successfully taught to the members in rote fashion. Scripture readings from the New Jerusalem Bible were used to set the scenes and to highlight the deep religious meanings of the *Kolendy*.

This nativity play can be staged by English-speaking people of Polish heritage, in their parishes or clubs. It can also be performed by Polish-speaking people who are studying English, particularly by those in middle schools or in high schools.

The following chapters are presented:

____ Introduction. Summary of how, where, and why this nativity play was written in 1989 and produced on December 14, 1989. It also describes where this nativity play might be used in the future. *Kolendy* are Polish Christmas carols.

____ Frontispiece: The "Featured" Kolendy. This chapter outlines the Polish *Kolendy* and hymns used in the play, and gives an interpretation on how each of the "featured" *Kolendy*/hymns work together to relate the nativity miracle.

____ Nativity Play: The Christmas Miracle in *Kolendy*. The play employs two readers, reading Bible verses from the New Jerusalem Bible (NJB) to set scenes. It also uses two interpreters to impart the literal meaning of the *Kolendy*/hymns, before they are sung in Polish by the actors and singers: Mary, Joseph, angels, shepherds, kings, and carolers. A soloist among the carolers is recommended for the hymns of the interlude.

A statue is used for baby Jesus; sheep, camels, and optional draft animals are statues or cardboard cutouts. Costumes can feature dress clothes in color hues (e.g., brown for Joseph, blue and white for Mary, white for angels, khaki for shepherds, wine for kings, and carolers can wear coats). More elaborate costumes for all could, of course, be used.

____ Lyrics and Actions. In this chapter, the Polish *Kolendy*/hymns are written in syllable format, for ease in learning them and do-able by rote. Actions to be performed, and who is to be singing, are annotated in this section.

____ Music Scores. In this chapter, the music scores for the Polish *Kolendy*/hymns and usually two verses of lyrics are given. Although the play uses only the first verses for most of the *Kolendy*/hymns to give a medley atmosphere, in a few places more verses were purposefully employed. Also, for most of the *Kolendy*/hymns, having more verses available and for the most part, having English translations, can make this section useful for other purposes such as caroling.

Frontispiece: The "Featured" *Kolendy*

Announcing the "Triumphant" Tidings

"Dzisiaj w Betlejem"	-	Today, in Bethlehem,
		Christ is born!

An "Awareness" Medley

"Wśród Nocnej Ciszy" (vs. 1)	-	Arise, shepherds! Hasten to
		Bethlehem to greet the Lord!
"Bracia, Patrzcie Jeno"	-	What's going on in Bethlehem?
"Gdy Się Chrystus Rodzi"	-	Christ is born:
		"Glory to God in the highest!"
"Bóg Się Rodzi"	-	"The Word was made flesh
		And dwelt amongst us."
"Wesołą Nowinę"	-	Listen brothers and sisters,
		To the joyful tidings!
		Where is the child?

A "Miracle" Medley

"Wśród Nocnej Ciszy" (vs. 2)	-	The shepherds found the child,
		Lying in a manger.
"Cicha Noc"	-	Silent night.
"Mędrcy Świata Monarchowie"	-	Wise men, kingmakers, where are
		You hurrying to give honor?
"O Józefie"	-	Questioning Joseph:
		"Where was Jesus born?"

[Interlude—"How Can This Be?"]

"Archanioł Boży Gabriel"	-	The angel Gabriel was sent to
		The virgin Mary: "Hail Mary,
		Full of grace, the Lord is with you!"
"Uwielbiaj Duszo Moja"	-	*The Magnificat:*
		"My soul doth magnify the Lord"

"Honoring" Mary and "Treasuring" the Infant, Jesus

"Śliczna Panienka"	-	Honoring Mary, mother of Jesus,
		Who "laid Jesus on straw like a lily,"
"Lulajże Jezuniu"	-	Treasuring the infant, Jesus,
		"Pearl very precious."

"Honoring" the Infant, Jesus

"Wśród Nocnej Ciszy" (vs. 3)	-	Greetings to our Savior,
		Foretold in ages past.
"W Żłobie Leży"	-	Jesus Christ is sent to us today,
		As an infant in a manger.
		Let us worship him as Lord and King.

Nativity Play:
The Christmas Miracle in *Kolendy*

Announcing "Triumphant" Tidings

Reader 1	-	Isaiah 7:14 (NJB)
		The Lord will give you a sign in any case: It is this: the young woman is with child and will give birth to a son whom she will call Immanuel.
Reader 2	-	Luke 2:11 (NJB)
		Today in the town of David a Saviour has been born to you; he is Christ the Lord.
Interpreter 1	-	Today in Bethlehem, we have heard the glad tidings
		that the Virgin Mary brought forth the Son of God!
Interpreter 2	-	Christ is born!
		He liberates us!
		Angels are playing,
		kings are greeting,
		shepherds are singing,
		animals are kneeling;
		all are proclaiming a miracle!
Singers	-	Vs. 1: "Dzisiaj w Betlejem" (Lyrics #1)

An "Awareness" Medley

Reader 1	-	Luke 2:1–7 (NJB)
		Now it happened that at this time Caesar Augustus issued a decree that a census should be made of the whole inhabited world.
		This census—the first—took place while Quirinius was governor of Syria, and everyone went to be registered, each to his own town.
		So Joseph set out from the town of Nazareth in Galilee for Judaea, to David's town called Bethlehem, since he was of David's House and line, in order to be registered together with Mary, his betrothed, who was with child.
		Now it happened that, while they were there, the time came for her to have her child, and she gave birth to a son, her first-born. She wrapped him in swaddling clothes and laid him in a manger because there was no room for them in the living-space.
Reader 2	-	Luke 2:8–20 (NJB)
		In the countryside close by there were shepherds out in the fields keeping guard over their sheep during the watches of the night.
		An angel of the Lord stood over them and the glory of the Lord shone round them. They were terrified, but the angel said, "Do not be afraid. Look, I bring you news of great joy, a joy to be shared by the whole people. Today in the town of David a Saviour has been born to you; he is Christ the Lord. And here is a sign for you: you will find a baby wrapped in swaddling clothes and lying in a manger."
		And all at once with the angel there was a great throng of the hosts of heaven, praising God with the words: Glory to God in the highest heaven, and on earth peace for those he favours.

		Now it happened that when the angels had gone from them into heaven, the shepherds said to one another, "Let us go to Bethlehem and see this event which the Lord has made known to us." So they hurried away and found Mary and Joseph, and the baby lying in the manger. When they saw the child they repeated what they had been told about him, and everyone who heard it was astonished at what the shepherds said to them. As for Mary, she treasured all these things and pondered them in her heart. And the shepherds went back glorifying and praising God for all they had heard and seen, just as they had been told.
Interpreter 1	-	In the midst of the quiet night,
		all are becoming aware.
Interpreter 2	-	Get up, shepherds!
		God is born for you this day!
		Get yourselves together as soon as possible
		and hasten to Bethlehem
		to welcome the Lord!
Singers	-	Vs. 1: "Wśród Nocnej Ciszy" (Lyrics #2.1)
Interpreter 1	-	But friends! Look over there!
		Look how the heavens are on fire!
		It is sure that something wondrous
		is going on in Bethlehem!
Interpreter 2	-	Let's abandon our homes and our valuable herds.
		Let's let our Lord God watch over them,

		and we, we'll go to Bethlehem!
Singers	-	Vs. 1: "Bracia, Patrzcie Jeno" (Lyrics #3.)
Reader 1	-	Luke 2:14 (NJB)
		Glory to God in the highest heaven, and on earth peace for those he favours.
Interpreter 1	-	Christ is born and comes on earth;
		a dark night flounders in a ray of light!
Interpreter 2	-	The angels are rejoicing. They are singing in the high heavens,
		"Gloria in Excelsis Deo."
Singers	-	Vs. 1: "Gdy Się Chrystus Rodzi" (Lyrics #4)
Interpreter 1	-	God is born on earth,
		and earthly powers tremble!
		God is brought down from heavenly splendor.
		His light is lit; earthly grandeur fades!
		His kingdom is without end!
Interpreter 2	-	Humbled yet clothed in radiant glory!
		A mortal, yet our Lord forever!
		"The Word was made flesh and dwelt amongst us."
Singers	-	Vs. 1: "Bóg Się Rodzi" (Lyrics #5)
Interpreter 1	-	Friends, listen to the joyful tidings.
		Let's welcome this heavenly Child.
		What good news this is!

Interpreter 2	-	Tell me: where is this Child,
		so we can go there quickly
		to see Him!
Singers	-	Vs. 1: "Wesołą Nowinę" (Lyrics #6)

A "Miracle" Medley

Reader 1	-	Luke 2:12 (NJB)
		And here is a sign for you: you will find a baby wrapped in swaddling clothes and lying in a manger.
Reader 2	-	Luke 2:16–18 (NJB)
		So they hurried away and found Mary and Joseph, and the baby lying in the manger. When they saw the child they repeated what they had been told about him, and everyone who heard it was astonished at what the shepherds said to them.
Interpreter 1	-	They went and found the Child in the manger
		with all the signs that had been described.
Interpreter 2	-	They gave Him honor as to God
		and welcomed Him
		with great joy!
Singers	-	"Poszli Znależli" (Lyrics #2.2)
		(vs. 2: "Wśród Nocnej Ciszy")
Interpreter 1	-	Silent night, holy night;
		all is calm, all is bright!
Interpreter 2	-	Joseph keeps watch with Mary
		while God's Child
		sleeps in heavenly peace!
Singers	-	Vs. 1: "Cicha Noc" (Lyrics #7)
Reader 1	-	Matthew 2:1–12 (NJB)

		After Jesus had been born at Bethlehem in Judaea during the reign of King Herod, suddenly some wise men came to Jerusalem from the east asking, "Where is the infant king of the Jews? We saw his star as it rose and have come to do him homage." When King Herod heard this he was perturbed, and so was the whole of Jerusalem. He called together all the chief priests and the scribes of the people, and enquired of them where the Christ was to be born. They told him, "At Bethlehem in Judaea, for this is what the prophet wrote: And you, Bethlehem, in the land of Judah, you are by no means the least among the leaders of Judah, for from you will come a leader who will shepherd my people Israel." Then Herod summoned the wise men to see him privately. He asked them the exact date on which the star had appeared and sent them on to Bethlehem with the words, "Go and find out all about the child, and when you have found him, let me know, so that I too may go and do him homage." Having listened to what the king had to say, they set out. And suddenly the star they had seen rising went forward and halted over the place where the child was. The sight of the star filled them with delight, and going into the house they saw the child with his mother Mary, and falling to their knees, they did him homage. Then, opening their treasures, they offered him gifts of gold and frankincense and myrrh. But they were given a warning in a dream not to go back to Herod, and returned to their own country by a different way.
Interpreter 1	-	Wise men, kingmakers,
		to whom are you hastening to give honor?

		Tell us now:
		Do you wish to see the Child?
Interpreter 2	-	He, in the manger, has no throne
		and wields no scepter!
		But the prophecy of His destined departure from life
		is already being spread on the earth!
Singers	-	Vs. 1: "Mędrcy Świata Monarchowie" (Lyrics #8)
Reader 2	-	Matthew 1:18–25 (NJB)
		This is how Jesus Christ came to be born. His mother Mary was betrothed to Joseph; but before they came to live together she was found to be with child through the Holy Spirit.

Her husband Joseph, being an upright man and wanting to spare her disgrace, decided to divorce her informally.

He had made up his mind to do this when suddenly the angel of the Lord appeared to him in a dream and said, "Joseph son of David, do not be afraid to take Mary home as your wife, because she has conceived what is in her by the Holy Spirit.

"She will give birth to a son and you must name him Jesus, because he is the one who is to save his people from their sins."

Now all this took place to fulfill what the Lord had spoken through the prophet: Look! The virgin is with child and will give birth to a son whom they will call Immanuel, a name which means "God-is-with-us."

When Joseph woke up he did what the angel of the Lord had told him to do: he took his wife to his home; he had not had intercourse with her when she gave birth to a son; and he named him Jesus. |
| | | |

Interpreter 2	-	Oh Joseph!
Interpreter 1	-	What can I do for you?
Interpreter 2	-	Tell us where Jesus was born!
Interpreter 1	-	In Bethlehem!
Interpreter 2	-	Praise to You, Lord Jesus Christ,
		for Your chaste birth
		in Bethlehem!
Singers	-	Vs. 1: "O Jósefie" (Lyrics #9)

[Interlude: "How Can This Be?"]

Reader 1	-	Luke 1:26–38 (NJB)
		In the sixth month the angel Gabriel was sent by God to a town in Galilee called Nazareth, to a virgin betrothed to a man named Joseph, of the House of David; and the virgin's name was Mary. He went in and said to her, "Rejoice, you who enjoy God's favour! The Lord is with you." She was deeply disturbed by these words and asked herself what this greeting could mean, but the angel said to her, "Mary, do not be afraid; you have won God's favour. "Look! You are to conceive in your womb and bear a son, and you must name him Jesus. He will be great and will be called Son of the Most High. The Lord God will give him the throne of his ancestor David; he will rule over the House of Jacob for ever and his reign will have no end." Mary said to the angel, "But how can this come about, since I have no knowledge of man?" The angel answered, "The Holy Spirit will come upon you, and the power of the Most High will cover you with its shadow. And so the child will be holy and will be called Son of God. "And I tell you this too: your cousin Elizabeth also, in her old age, has conceived a son, and she whom people called barren is now in her sixth month, for nothing is impossible to God." Mary said, "You see before you the Lord's servant, let it happen to me as you have said." And the angel left her.
Interpreter 1	-	Gabriel, an archangel of God, was sent to the Virgin Mary
		From the majesty of the Holy Trinity,
		And, in this manner, discharged the legation of God:

Interpreter 2	-	"Hail Mary, Full of Grace, The Lord is with Thee."
Soloist	-	Vs. 1: "Archanioł Boży Gabryel" (Lyrics #10)
Reader 2	-	Luke 1: 39–45 NJB
		Mary set out at that time and went as quickly as she could into the hill country to a town in Judah. She went into Zechariah's house and greeted Elizabeth. Now it happened that as soon as Elizabeth heard Mary's greeting, the child leapt in her womb, and Elizabeth was filled with the Holy Spirit. She gave a loud cry and said, "Of all women you are the most blessed, and blessed is the fruit of your womb. Why should I be honoured with a visit from the mother of my Lord? Look, the moment your greeting reached my ears, the child in my womb leapt for joy. Yes, blessed is she who believed that the promise made her by the Lord would be fulfilled."
Interpreter 1	-	Luke 1: 46–50 NJB.
		And Mary said: "My soul proclaims the greatness of the Lord and my spirit rejoices in God my Saviour; because he has looked upon the humiliation of his servant. Yes, from now onwards all generations will call me blessed, for the Almighty has done great things for me. Holy is his name, and his faithful love extends age after age to those who fear him."
Interpreter 2	-	Luke 1: 51–55 NJB.
		He has used the power of his arm, he has routed the arrogant of heart. He has pulled down princes from their thrones and raised high the lowly. He has filled the starving with good things, sent the rich away empty.

		He has come to the help of Israel his servant, mindful of his faithful love —according to the promise he made to our ancestors—of his mercy to Abraham and to his descendants forever.
Soloist	-	"Uwielbiaj Duszo Moja" (Lyrics #11)

"Honoring" Mary and "Treasuring" the Infant, Jesus

Interpreter 1	-	A lovely young lady brought forth Jesus,
		And covered Him with hay, in the airy stable.
Interpreter 2	-	It was hay like a lily
		On which Mary placed Jesus.
Singers	-	Vs. 1: "Śliczna Panienka" (Lyrics #12)
Interpreter 1	-	Sleep now, dear Jesus, my precious pearl!
		Sleep now, dear Jesus, my precious one!
Interpreter 2	-	Sleep now, dear Jesus, sleep, sleep,
		And you, His tearful mother, hug Him!
Singers	-	Vs. 1: "Lulajże Jezuniu" (Lyrics #13)

"Honoring" the Infant, Jesus

Interpreter 1	-	Welcome, Savior, whom we have needed for so many ages!
		You have been expected for so many thousands of years!
Interpreter 2	-	For You, kings and prophets
		Have waited. And You, this night,
		Have revealed Yourself to us!
Singers	-	"Ach Witaj Zbawco!" (Lyrics #2.3)
		(Vs. 3: "Wśród Nocnej Ciszy")
Interpreter 1	-	He lies in a manger—who will hasten
		To sing *kolendy* to the little One,
		Jesus Christ,
		Who was sent to us today!?
Interpreter 2	-	Shepherds, come and
		Play for Him with gratefulness.
		Give honor to our Lord!
Singers	-	Vs. 1: "W Żłobie Leży" (Lyrics #14)

Lyrics and Actions

Announcing "Triumphant" Tidings

1. "Dzisiaj w Betlejem" (Music #1)

Vs. 1:	Joseph and Mary sit in chairs near *żłóbek*, or manger; rest stand around *żłóbek*. All sing.
Dzi – siaj w Bet – le – jem, Dzi – siaj w Bet – le – jem, We – so – ł a No – wi – na! Że Pan – na czys – ta, Że Pan – na czys – ta, Po – ro – dzi – ła Sy – na.	
Chorus:	Joseph stops singing.
Chrys – tus się ro – dzi,	Joseph considers the miracle.
Nas Os – wo – bo – dzi,	Joseph stands up.
A – nie – li gra – ją,	Joseph gestures to the angels, leaving for upper middle left.
Kró – le wi – ta – ją,	Joseph gestures to the wise men, leaving for upper right stage.
Pas – te – rze śpie – wa – ją,	Joseph gestures to the shepherds, leaving for lower left stage.
By – dlę – ta klę – ka – ją,	Joseph takes up and arranges a sheep. Carolers move to upper middle right of stage.
Cu – da, cu – da! O – gła – sza – ją.	Joseph sits down and reflects, while singing this line.
Repeat chorus	All sing.

An "Awareness" Medley

2.1. "Wśród Nocnej Ciszy" (Music #2)

Vs. 1:	Carolers sing.
Wśród noc – nej ci – szy, Głos się roz – cho – dzi, Wstań – cie pa – ste – rze, Bóg się wam ro – dzi .	Angels turn toward shepherds. Angels sing. Carolers sing softer.
Chorus:	
Czym prę – dzej się wy – bie – raj – cie, Do Be – tle – jem po – spie – szaj – cie, Przy – wi – tać Pa – na!	
Repeat chorus	

3. "Bracia, Patrzcie Jeno" (Music #3)

Vs. 1:	
Bra – cia patrz - cie je – no, Jak nie – bo go – re – je . Znać że coś dzi – wne – go W Be – tle – jem się dzie – je.	Shepherds at lower left of stage. Shepherd 1 sings. Carolers sing softer.
Chorus:	
Rzuć – my bu – dy, war – ty sta – da, Nie – chaj nie – mi, Pan Bóg wła – da, A my do Be – tle – jem, A my do Be – tle – jem, Do Be – tle – jem.	Shepherds 2 and 3 sing. Carolers sing softer.

4. "Gdy Się Chrystus Rodzi" (Music #4)

End of chorus:	
Glo – r i – a, glo – r i – a, glo – r i – a, in ex – cel – sis De – o !	Angels sing in harmony.
Vs. 1:	
Gdy się Chry – stus ro – dzi, I na świat. przy – cho – dzi, Ciem – na noc w jas – no – sci pro – mie – ni – stej bro – dzi.	All sing, except angels.
Chorus:	
A – nio – ł o – wie się ra – du – ją Pod nie – bio – sy wy – spie – wu – ją: Glo – r i – a, glo – r i – a, glo – r i – a, in ex – cel – sis De – o !	 Angels sing in harmony.
Repeat chorus	

5. "Bóg Się Rodzi" (Music #5)

Vs. 1:	Wise men at upper right of stage. Wise men sing. Carolers sing softer.
Bóg się ro – dzi, moc tru – chle – je, Pan nie – bio – sów o – bna – żo – ny, O – gień krze – pnie, blask ciem - nie – je, Ma gra – ni – ce Nie – skoń – czo – ne.	
Chorus:	
Wsgar – dzo – ny o – kry – ty chwa – łą, Śmier – tel – ny król nad wie – ka – mi ; A Sło – wo Cia – łem się sta – ł o, I mie – szka – ło mię – dzy na – mi .	
Repeat chorus	

6. "Wesołą Nowinę" (Music #6)

Vs. 1:	Shepherds lower left of stage
We – so – łą no – wi – nę bra – cia słu – chaj – cie, Nie – bie – ską Dzie – ci – nę ze mną wi – taj – cię.	Shepherd 1 sings. Carolers sing softer.
Chorus:	
Jak mi – ła ta no – wi – na Mów, gdzie jest ta dzie – ci – na ? Byś – my tam po – bie – że – li I uj – rze – li !	Shepherds 2 and 3 sing. Carolers sing softer.
Repeat chorus	All move toward *żłóbek* again, except wise men: Angels to back left. Carolers to back right. Shepherds to left front.

A "Miracle" Medley

2.2.   "Poszli Znaleźli," vs. 2: "Wśród Nocnej Ciszy" (Music #2)

Vs. 2:	Carolers sing.
Posz – li zna – leź – li, Dzie – cią – tko w zło – bie, Z wszy – stki – mi zna – ki, da – ny – mi So – bie .	
Chorus:	
Ja – ko Bo – gu cześć Mu da – li, A wi – ta – jąc za – wo – ła – li Z wiel – kiej ra – do – ści !	
Repeat chorus	

7.   "Cicha Noc" (Music #7)

Vs. 1:	Angels and shepherds sing. Carolers sing softer.
Ci – cha noc, Świę – ta noc ! Wszy – stko śpi, a to ni Czu – wa Jó – sef z Ma – ry – ą, Kie – dy Bos – ka Dzie – ci – na w bło – gim spo – ko – ju śpi ! w bło – gim spo – ko – ju śpi .	

8. "Mędrcy Świata Monarchowie" (Music #8)

Vs. 1:	Wise men move slowly, halfway to right front stage. All but wise men sing.
Mędr – cy świa – ta, mo – nar – cho – wie, Gdzie spiesz – nie dą – ży – cie ? Po – wiedz – cież nam, trzej kró – lo – wie, Chce – cie wi – dzieć Dzie – cię ?	
Chorus:	
O – no w zło – bie, nie ma tro – nu, Ni ber – ła nie dzie – rzy, A pro – ro – ctwo Je – go zgo – nu Już się w świe – cię sze – rzy .	
Repeat chorus	

9. "O Jósefie" (Music #9)

Vs. 1:	Wise men move to right front.
O Jó – se – fie !	Wise men sing.
Cze – go chce – cie ?	Joseph sings.
Po – wiedz –że nam gdzie Się Chry - stus na – ro – dził !	Wise men sing.
W Be – tle – jem, w Be – tle – jem !	Joseph sings.
Chorus:	All sing.
Chwa – ła to – bie Je –zu Chry – ste, Za twe na – ro – dze – nie czy – ste, W Be – tle – jem .	

[Interlude: "How Can This Be?]

10. "Archanioł Boży Gabryel" (Music #10)

Vs. 1:	Mary goes to right of stage. Gabriel and another angel walk over to right of stage. Soloist sings.
Arch – an – ioł Bo – ży Ga – bry – el Pos – łan do Pan – ny Ma – ry – i .	
Chorus:	
Z ma – jes – ta –tu Trój – cy Świę – tej, Tak spra – wo – wał po – sel – stwo k 'Niej : Zdro – was Pan – no, Łaś – kiś peł – na Pan jest z To – bą, to rzecz pew – na.	
Repeat chorus	Carolers join soloist in singing.
	Angels return to their choir. Mary turns toward center stage and is still and statuesque.

11. "Uwielbiaj Duszo Moja" (Music #11)

Vs. 1–4:	Soloist chants verses 1–4 of *The Magnificat* in Polish. Mary remains still and statuesque.
Uwielbiaj duszo Moja sławę Pana Mego Chwal Boga Stworzyczela tak bardzo dobrego.	
Bóg Mój, zbawienie Moje, jedyna otucha, Bóg Mi rozkoszą serca i weselem ducha.	
Bo mile przyjąć raczył Swej sługi pokorę, Łaskawem okiem wejrzał na Dawida córe.	
Przeto wszystkie narody co ziemie osiędą, Odtąd błogosławioną Mnie nazywać będą.	

"Honoring" Mary and "Treasuring" the Infant, Jesus

12. "Śliczna Panienka" (Music #12)

Vs. 1:	Mary slowly returns to her place and is seated. All sing except Mary.
Śli – czna Pa – nien – ka, Je – zu – są zro – dzi – ła, W staj – ni po – wi – wszy, Sian – kiem go na – kry – ła.	
Chorus:	Mary gets up and arranges Jesus on hay.
O śia – no, śia – no, Śia – no jak li – li –ja, Na któ – rem kła – dzie Je – zu – sa Ma – ry – a .	
Repeat chorus	

13. "Lulajże Jezuniu" (Music #13)

Vs. 1:	All sing.
Lu – laj – że Je – zu – niu, mo – ja pe – reł – ko, Lu – laj – że Je – zu – niu, me pie – ści – deł – ko.	
Chorus:	
Lu – laj – że Je – zu – niu, lu – laj – że, lu – laj, A Ty Go Ma – tu – chno w pła – czu u – tu – laj .	
Repeat chorus	

Honoring the Infant, Jesus

2.3."Ach Witaj, Zbawco," vs. 3: "Wśród Nocnej Ciszy" (Music #2)

Vs. 3:	Carolers sing.
"Ach wi – taj, Zbaw – co z daw – na żą – da – ny, Ty – le ty – się – cy lat wy – glą – da – ny !	
Chorus:	
Na Cie – bie kró – le, pro – ro – cy Cze – ka – li, a Tyś tej no – cy Nam się ob – ja – wił ."	
Repeat chorus	

14. "W Żłobie Leży" (Music #14)

Vs. 1:	All sing, standing around *żłóbek*.
W zło – bie le – ży ! któż po – bie – ży Ko – lę – do – wać ma – łe – mu Je – zu – so –wi Chry – stu – so – wi Dziś do nas że – sła – ne – mu ?	
Chorus:	
Pa – stu – szko –wie przy – by – waj – cie, Je – mu wdzię – cznie przy – gry – waj – cie, Ja – ko Pa – nu na – sze – mu.	
Repeat chorus	

Music Scores

Musician Notes

1. Today In Bethlehem

Dzisiaj w Betlejem

Music Arr. - Rose Polski Anderson

English Version - Cecily Kowalewska Helgesen

2. Sweet Virgin Mary, sweet Virgin Mary
O'er her Wee Babe bending,
And kindly Joseph, and kindly Joseph
Gently them attending. CHORUS:

2. *Marya Panna, Marya Panna,*
Dzieciątko piastuje,
I Jósef stary, i Jósef stary,
On Je Pielęgnuje. CHOR:

Reprinted by permission of Immigration Histroy Research Center Archives, University of Minnesota

Musician Notes

2. In the Still of the Night

Old Christmas Carol

Wsrod Nocnej Ciszy

English version-Edmund Lukaszewski
CarolMusic Arr.- Adam Harasowski

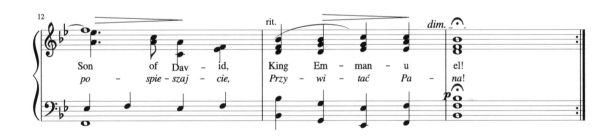

2. They found the Saviour with His Mother mild,
    Laid in the manger, Infant Jesus Child.
|: Bow ye shepherds to the Christ King,
    Bring to Him your humble offering,
    King Emmanuel!

3. "Ah, welcome Saviour, whom *
    we've long desired,
    For many long years, man for
    thee aspired;
|: Kings and prophets waited for
    thee;
    Thou this night to us unworthy,
    Kingly dost appear."   :|

2. *Poszli, znaleźli, Dzieciątko w żtobie,*
    Z wszystkimi znaki danymi Sobie.
|: *Jako Bogu cześć Mu dali,*
    A witając, zawołali
    Z wielkiej radości! :|

3. *"Ach witaj, Zbawco z dawna żądany,* *
    Tyle tysięcy lat wyglądany!
|: *Na Ciebie króle, prorocy*
    Czekali, a Tyś tej nocy
    Nam się objawił. " :|

* Public Domain.

Reprinted by permission of Immigration History Research Center Archives, University of Minnesota.

Musician Notes

3. Brothers, Look There Yonder

Music Arr. - Edmund Contoski

Bracia, Patrzcie Jeno

English version - Josepha Contoski

Broth – ers look there yon – der! Skies a-flame! O won–der Ver – y strange the to – ken
Bra – cia, patr zcie je – no, Jak nie – bo go – re – je. Znać że coś dzi – wne–go

O'er the town Beth – le hem. We must leave huts, sheep and ox–en, Lord over them will
w Be tle – jem się dzie – je. Rzuć – my bu–dy, war – ty sta–da, Nie chaj nie – mi

keep on wat ching While we go to Beth-le-hem. We go to Beth – le – hem, to Beth-le – hem,
Pan Bóg wła–da, A – my do Be-tle-jem. a my do Be – tle jem, do Be-tle – jem,

2. Brother, see the great star,
Spreading out its rays far.
Surely, it is gracing
God, in its swift racing
With bold steps we hasten to Him,
Filled with joy, we'll bow before Him,
Son of God in Bethlehem.
God's Son in Bethlehem, in Bethlehem.

3. Little town Bethlehem,
Brings to Juda great fame
Everywhere remembered,
By all countries honored.
Let joy fill our hearts mankind,
As we worship Him we find,
In a manger, in Bethlehem,
Manger in Bethlehem, in Bethlehem.

Reprinted by permission of Immigration History Research Center Archives, University of Minnesota.

Musician Notes

4. Christ, the King, is Born

Gdy Sie Chrystus Rodzi

Music Arr. - Adam Harasowski

English version - Cecily Kowalewska Helgesen

Christ, the King, is born,— On an ear-ly morn,— Ra-diant glows the dark— night,
Gdy się Chry-stus ro-dzi, I na świat przy-cho-dzi, Ciem-na noc w jas-no-ści

Skies a-flame with bright— light, All the an-gels are re-joic-ing Heav-en-ly mu-sic, they are voic-ing,
pro-mie-ni-stej bro-dzi, A,-nio-ło-wie się ra-du-ją Pod nie-bio-sy wy-śpie-wu-ją:

Glo-ri-a, glo-ri-a, glo-ri-a, in ex-cel-sis De-—o!
Glo-ri-a, glo-ri-a, glo-ri-a, in ex-cel-sis De-—o!

2. Angels told the shepherds,
   Keeping watch o'er their herds,
   "Follow ye the bright star,
   Bethlehem is not far,
   |: For the Savior there is born,
   To the world this early morn,
   Gloria, gloria, gloria in excelsis Deo!" :|

2. *Mówią do pasterzy, którzy*
   trzód swych strzegli,
   Aby do Betlejem czem prędzej
   pobiegli,
   |: *Bo się narodził Zbawiciel,*
   wzego świata Odkupiciel,
   Gloria, gloria, gloria, in excelsis Deo! :|

Musician Notes

5. God Is Born
Bóg Się Rodzi

Traditional Polish Air
English version - Cecily Kowalewska Helgesen
Music Arr. - Rose Polski Anderson

God is born on earth, powers trem - ble,__ Lord be - reft of heav' nly splen - dor,
Bóg się ro - dzi, moc tru - chle - je, Pan, nie - bio - sów o - bna żo - ny,

Lust rous flames fade, fires dis sem ble, In - fin - ite un - end - ing Won - der! Scorned yet clothed in
O - gień krze - pnie, blask ciem - nie - je, Ma gra - ni - ce Nie - skoń - czo - ne. Wsgar - dzo - ny, o -

rad iant glo - ry, Mor - tal though He is Lord Je - sus, Thus the Word be - came the flesh
kry - ty chwa - łą, Śmier - tel - ny Król nad wie - ka - mi; A Sło - wo Cia - łem się sta - ło,

Dwell - ing with out end a - mong us!
I mie - szka - ło mię - dzy na - mi.

2. Why leave heaven for this bleak earth,
Heaven bright in all its glory,
To dwell humbly from day of birth,
To fufill the prophet's story.
Lo, He suffered through our folly,
Mortal, though He is Lord Jesus,
Thus the Word became the Flesh
Dwelling without end among us!

2. *Coż masz niebo nad ziemiany?*
Bóg porzucił szczęście twoje,
Wszedł między lud ukochany
Dzieląc znim trudy i znoje:
Nie mało cierpiał, nie mało,
Żeśmy byli winni sami.
A Słowo Ciałem się stało
I mieszkało między nami!

Reprinted by permission of Immigration History Research Center Archives, University of Minnesota.

Musician Notes

6. Joyful Tidings
Wesołą Nowinę

English version - Lucille Jasinski

Music Arr. - Stanislaw Siedlewski

Har-ken to joyful tid-ings Oh shep-herds, list - en, Let us this
We - so - łą no - wi - nę bra - cia słu - chaj - cie, Nie - bie - sĸą

heav'nly In - fant A - dore and greet Him. Where is this
Dzie - ci - nę ze - mną wi - taj - cie. Jaĸ mi - ła,

blessed stran - ger Born in a low-ly man - ger? Hast - en this
ta no - wi - na Mów, gdzie jest ta dzie-ci - na? Byś - my tam

ho - ly night, to the won - drous sight!
po - bie - że - li I uj - rze - li!

Reprinted by permission of Immigration History Research Center Archives, University of Minnesota.

Musician Notes

7. Silent Night

Cicha Noc

Ci - cha noc, świę - ta noc! Wszystko śpi, a - to-li

Czu - wa Jó - zef z Ma - ry - ą, Kie - dy Bos - ka Dzie - ci - na

w bło - gim spo - ko-ju śpi! W bło - gim spo - ko-ju śpi.

2. Cicha noc, święta noc!
   Tobie cześć chcemy nieść,
   Boś pastuszkom oznajmiony,
   Przez Anielskie Gloria,
   /Jezu, witamy Cię!/

3. Cicha noc, święta noc!
   Boże nasz, serca masz,
   Radość sprawia nam nowina,
   Że nadeszła ta godzina,
   /W którejś narodził się./

1. Silent night, holy night,
   All is calm, all is bright
   'Round yon Virgin Mother and Child.
   Holy Infant, so tender and mild,
   Sleep in heavenly peace,
   Sleep in heavenly peace.

2. Silent night, holy night,
   Shepherds quake at the sight;
   Glories stream from heaven afar,
   Heav'nly hosts sing alleluia;
   Christ, the Savior is born,
   Christ, the Savior is born!

3. Silent night, holy night,
   Son of God, love's pure light,
   Radiant, beams from thy holy face.
   With the dawn of redeeming grace,
   Jesus, Lord, at Thy birth,
   Jesus, Lord, at Thy birth!

Musician Notes

8. Three Good Wise Men
Mędcry Świata

Music Arr. - Adam Harasowski

English version - Cecily Kowalewska Helgesen

2. Three good wise men, malice fearful
Persecutes the new King,
Tidings dismal, tidings dreadful,
Herod is conspiring.
Yet the monarchs will not frighten,
To Bethlehem hasten,
While the star proclaims the Savior,
Life and Hope Redeemer!

Reprinted by permission of Immigration History Research Center Archives, University of Minnesota.

Musician Notes

9. O Joseph! What Are You Asking?

O Józefie! Czego Chcecie?

Ask. O Jò - ze-fie! *Joseph.* Cze - go chce-cie? *Ask.* Powiedzże nam gdzie się Chry stus na-ro - dzil?

Joseph. W Betle, - jem W Betle - jem. *All.* Chwała to-bie Je-zu Chryste, za twe na - ro - dze nie czy ste,

W Be - tle - jem.

1. O Józefie!
 - Czego chcecie?
 Powiedzże nam, gdzie się Chrystus narodził?
 - Betlejem, w Betlejem!
  Chwała Tobie Jezu Chryste,
  Za Twe narodzenie czyste
  W Betlejem!

2. O Józefie!
 - Czego chcecie?
 Powiedzże nam, kto Jezusa powijał?
 - Maryja, Maryja.
  Chwała Tobie i t.d.

3. O Józefie!
 - Czego chcecie?
 Powiedzże nam, kto Jezusa kołysał?
 - Ja Jósef, ja Józef.
  Chwała Tobie i t.d.

4. O Józefie!
 - Czego chcecie?
 Powiedzże nam, kto Jezusowi śpiewał?
 - Anieli, Anieli.
  Chwała Tobie i t.d.

5. O Józefie!
 - Czego chcecie?
 Powiedzże nam, kto Jezusa zagrzewał?
 - Wół, osioł, wół, osioł.
  Chwała Tobie i t.d.

6. O Józefie!
 - Czego chcecie?
 Powiedzże nam, kto Mu pokłon oddawał?
 - Pasterze, Pasterze.
  Chwała Tobie i t.d.

7. O Józefie!
 - Czego chcecie?
 Powiedzże nam, kto Jezusa odwiedził?
 - Królowie, Królowie.
  Chwała Tobie i t.d.

8. O Józefie!
 - Czego chcecie?
 Powiedzże nam, kto Jezusa zabić chciał?
 - Król Heród, Król Heród.
  Chwała Tobie i t.d.

9. O Józefie!
 - Czego chcecie?
 Powiedzże nam, czemu Jezus ubogi?
 - Bo drogi, bo drogi.
  Chwała Tobie i t. d.

10. O Józefie!
 - Czego chcecie?
 Oto Ciebie z nabożeństwem prosimy;
 - A o co, a o co?
  Aby w raz z osobą twoją,
  Był nam Jezus Matką Swoją
  Przy śmierci.

Musician Notes

10. Archaniol Boży Gabryel

mf Arch an ioł Bo - ży Ga bry el Pos łan do Pan - ny Ma ry - i,

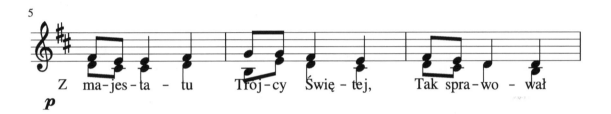

p Z ma - jes - ta - tu Trój - cy Świę - tej, Tak spra - wo - wał

po - sel - stwo k'Niej: Zdro waś Pan no, *f* łas kiś peł na,

Pan jest z To - bą to rzecz pew na.

2. Panna się wielce zdumiała,
   Z poselstwa, które słyszała;
   Pokorniuchno się skłoniła,
   Jako Panna świątobliwa;
   Zasmuciła się z tej mowy,
   Nic nie rzekła Aniołowi.

Musician Notes

11. Uwielbiaj Duszo Moja

The Magnificat - In Polish

Public Domain.

Uwielbiaj duszo moja sławę   Pa - na me - go   Chwal Boga Stworzy-
[ciela tak bar- dzo do - bre - go.

2. Bóg Mój, zbawienie Moje, jedyna otucha,
   Bóg Mi rozkoszą serca i weselem dueha.

3. Bo mile przyjąć raczył Swej sługi pokore,
   Łaskawem okiem wejrzał na Dawida córę

4. Przeto wszystkie narody, co ziemie osiędą,
   Odtąd błogosławioną Mnie nazywać będą.

5. Bo wielkimi darami uczczonam od Tego,
   Którego moc przedziwna, święte Imię Jego.

6. Którzy się Pana boją, szczęśliwi na wieki,
   Bo z nimi Miłosierdzie z rodu w ród daleki.

7. Na cały świat pokazał moc Swych ramion świętych,
   Rozprószył dumne myśli głów pychą nadętych.

8. Wyniosłych złożył z tronu, znikczemnił wielmożne,
   Wywyższył uwielmożnił w pokorę zamożne.

9. Głodnych nasycił hojnie i w dobra spanoszył,
   Bogaczów z torbą puścił i nędznie rozproszył.

10. Przyjął do łaski sługę Izraela cnego,
    Wspomniał nań użyczył mu miłosierdzia Swego.

11. Wypełnił, co był przyrzekł niegdyś ojcom naszym:
    Abrahamowi z potomstwem jego, wiecznym czasem.

12. Wszyscy śpiewajmy Bogu w Trójey jedynemu,
    Chwała Ojcu, Synowi, Duchowi Swiętemu.

13. Jak była na początku, tak zawsze niech będzie,
    Teraz i na wiek wieków niechaj słynie wszędzie.

The Magnificat - In English

1. My soul doth magnify the Lord.

2. And my spirit hath rejoiced in God my Savior.

3. Because He hath regarded the humility of His slave:

4. For behold from henceforth all generations shall call me blessed.

5. Because He that is mighty hath done great things to me; and holy in His name.

6. And His mercy is from generation unto generations, to them that fear Him.

7. He hath shewed might in His arm: He hath scattered the proud in the conceit of their heart.

8. He hath put down the mighty from their seat, and hath exalted the humble.

9. He hath filled the hungry with good things; and the rich He hath sent empty away.

10. He hath received Israel His servant, being mindful of His mercy:

11. As He spoke to our fathers, to Abraham and to his seed forever.

12. Glory be to the Father, and to the Son, and to the Holy Spirit,

13. As it was in the beginning, is now, and ever shall be, forever and ever, Amen.

Musician Notes

12. Fairest of Maidens
Śliczna Panienka

Arr. by Adam Harasowski

English Version by Cecily Kowalewska Helgesen

2. O why dear maiden,
Must He rest on poor hay?
O, pity maiden,
That the Babe should there lay.
|: O hay, most sweet hay,
Honored flower, holy,
It was upon thee
Jesus lay so lowly. :|

2. Czemuż litości
Nie masz Panno droga,
Żeś w liche siano,
Uwinęła Boga.
|: O siano, siano,
Siano kwiecie drogi,
Gdy się na tobie
Kładzie Bóg ubogi. :|

Musician Notes

13. Lullaby, Sweet Jesus
Lulajże, Jezuniu

Music Arr. - Rose Polski Anderson

English Version by Evelyn Cieslak

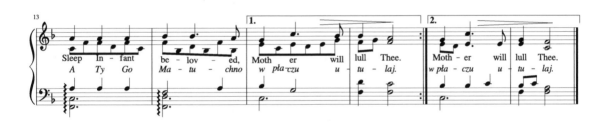

2. Close now Your wee eyelids, blinking
   with soft tears,
   Still Your wee lips trembling, for slumber
   time nears.
  |: Lullaby, sweet Jesus, lullaby, baby,
   Sleep Infant beloved, Mother will lull Thee.   :|

2. *Zamknijże znużone płaczem powieczki,*
   Utulże zemdlone lkaniem usteczki. Lulajże . . .
3. *Lulajże piekniuchny nasz Aniołeczku,*
   Lulajże wdziecniuchny świata Kwiateczku Lulajże . . .
4. *Lulajże Różyczko najozdobniejsza,*
   Lulajże Lilijko najprzyjemniejsza. Lulajże . . .

Reprinted by permission of Immigration History Research Center Archives, University of Minnesota.

Musician Notes

_____

_____

_____

_____

_____

_____

_____

_____

_____

_____

_____

_____

_____

_____

_____

14. In a Manger
W Żłobie Leży
Quartet

Peter Skarga (1536-1612)
English version - Zofia Kowalska McGinn
Music Arr. - Rose Polski Anderson

In a manger sleeps the In-fant, Has ten all to find Him there. Lit-tle Je-sus, to us
Wżło-bie le-ży! któż po-bie-ży Ko-lę-do-wać ma-łe-mu Je-zu-so-wi Chry-stu-

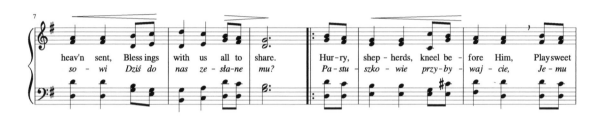

heav'n sent, Bless ings with us all to share. Hur-ry, shep-herds, kneel be-fore Him, Play sweet
so-wi Dziś do nas ze-sła-ne mu? Pa-stu-szko-wie przy-by-waj-cie, Je-mu

mu-sic like Se-ra-phim, Worship Him as Lord and King. Wor ship Him as Lord and King.
wdzię-cznie przy-gry-waj-cie, Ja-ko Pa-nu na-sze-mu, Ja-ko Pa-nu na sze-mu.

2. We shall follow, singing our song,
Bringing homage, gifts of prayer,
Little Saviour, bless this large throng,
Watch us with loving care.
|: Hurry, children, see Him sleeping,
Holy parents watch are keeping,
So let us all adore Him. :|

2. *My zaś sami z pionsneczkami*
Za wami pospieszymy,
A tak Tego Malehkiego
Niech wszyscy zobaczymy;
|: *Jak u bogo narodzony*
Płacze w stajni położony,
Więc go dziś ucieszymy. :|

Bibliography

Bible:

Excerpts from THE NEW JERUSALEM BIBLE published and copyright (c) 1985 by Darton, Longman & Todd and Doubleday, a division of Penguin Random House. Reprinted by permission.

Dictionary:

Kazimierz Bulas, Lawrence L. Thomas, Francis J. Whitfield, Kosciuszko Foundation, *The Kosciuszko Foundation* **Dictionary**: *English-Polish, Polish-English*. New York: Kosciuszko Foundation, 1986.

Music Scores (In performance order) for *Kolendy* and Hymns:

1. "Dzisiaj w Betlejem"

Polanie Club, *Treasured Polish Christmas Customs and Traditions*. Minneapolis, MN: Polanie Publishing, 1972, 72–73.

2.1. "Wśród Nocnej Ciszy"

Polanie Club, *Treasured Polish Christmas Customs and Traditions*. Minneapolis, MN: Polanie Publishing, 1972, 110.

3. "Bracia, Patrzcie Jeno"

Polanie Club, *Treasured Polish Christmas Customs and Traditions*. Minneapolis, MN: Polanie Publishing, 1972, 81.

4. "Gdy Się Chrystus Rodzi"

Polanie Club, *Treasured Polish Christmas Customs and Traditions*. Minneapolis, MN: Polanie Publishing, 1972, 86–87.

5. "Bóg Się Rodzi"

Polanie Club, *Treasured Polish Christmas Customs and Traditions*. Minneapolis, MN: Polanie Publishing, 1972, 92.

6. "Wesołą Nowinę"

Polanie Club, *Treasured Polish Christmas Customs and Traditions*. Minneapolis, MN: Polanie Publishing, 1972, 119.

2.2. "Poszli Znaleźli", vs. 2: "Wśród Nocnej Ciszy"

Polanie Club, *Treasured Polish Christmas Customs and Traditions*. Minneapolis, MN: Polanie Publishing, 1972, 110.

7. "Cicha Noc"

The Glory of God—Chwała Boża. Erie, PA: Vincentian Fathers Press (St. John Kanty Prep), 1967, 45–46.

8. "Mędrcy Świata Monarchowie"

Polanie Club, *Treasured Polish Christmas Customs and Traditions*. Minneapolis, MN: Polanie Publishing, 1972, 93.

9. "O Jósefie! Czego Chcecie?"

https://pl.wikisource.org/wiki/Pastora%C5%82ki_i_kol%C4%99dy/O_J%C3%B3zefie!_Czego_chcecie.

10. "Archanioł Boży Gabryel"

The Glory of God – Chwała Boża. Erie, PA: Vincentian Fathers Press (St. John Kanty Prep), 1967, 16.

11. "Uwielbiaj Duszo Moja"

The Magnificat in Polish: Hathi Trust Digital Library: Siedlecki, Jan, *Śpiewniczek Zawierający Pieśni Kościelne Z Melodyami Dla Użytku Wiernych*. Kraków, 1901, 448.

The Magnificat in English: http://www.traditioninaction.org/religious/b017rpMagnificat.htm.

12. "Śliczna Panienka"

Polanie Club,, *Treasured Polish Songs with English Translations*. Minneapolis, MN: Polanie Publishing, 1953, 215.

13. "Lulajże Jezuniu"

Polanie Club, *Treasured Polish Christmas Customs and Traditions*. Minneapolis, MN: Polanie Publishing, 1972, 118.

2.3."Ach Witaj Zbawco," vs. 3: "Wśród Nocnej Ciszy"

Polanie Club, *Treasured Polish Christmas Customs and Traditions*. Minneapolis, MN: Polanie Publishing, 1972, 110.

Added vs. 3 from:

The Glory of God—Chwała Boża. Erie, PA: Vincentian Fathers Press (St. John Kanty Prep), 1967, 24.

3. "Ach witaj, Zbawco z dawna żądany,
    Tyle tysięcy lat wyglądany!
|: Na Ciebie króle, prorocy
    Czekali, a Tyś tej nocy
    Nam się objawił.":|

Added vs. 3 translation by Msgr. John E. Ronan, from:

http://www.hymnsandcarolsofchristmas.com/Hymns_and_Carols/in_nights_deep_silence.htm.

3. "Ah, welcome Saviour, whom we've long desired,

For many long years, man for thee aspired;

|:   Kings and prophets waited for thee;
Thou this night to us unworthy,
Kingly dost appear." :|

14. "W Żłobie Leży"

Polanie Club, *Treasured Polish Christmas Customs and Traditions*. Minneapolis, MN: Polanie Publishing, 1972, 112–13.

Nativity Play Notes

Nativity Play Notes

About the Author

After her grade school years, Helen Gwozdz Miller graduated from St. Stanislaus Kostka School in Adams, Massachusetts. This is where she received her formal Polish education. (She later also studied Latin, French, and German.) After her high school years, she graduated from St. Joseph's High School in North Adams, Massachusetts. She graduated from Elms College in Chicopee, Massachusetts with a BA in mathematics and a minor in chemistry; she also studied philosophy and theology at the Elms. She has thirty graduate credits in mathematics at Fordham's Graduate School of Arts and Sciences.

She has been a parishioner in several Catholic parishes throughout her life, and is currently a parishioner at Our Lady of Lourdes, Whitehouse Station, New Jersey, where she has been for more than thirty-five years. She previously taught CCD there and was a member of the adult choir, and is currently a member of a women's spiritual reading and faith sharing group.

She is now retired, after a career in information technology.

She has three children and their spouses, and seven grandchildren, and resides with her husband, Frederick, in Clinton Township, New Jersey.

Printed in the United States
By Bookmasters